Greetings Cards

Annette Claxton

The Art of Crafts

First published in 1999 by
The Crowood Press Ltd
Ramsbury, Marlborough
Wiltshire SN8 2HR

The right of Annette Claxton to be identified as the author of this work has been asserted by her in accordance with the Copyright, Designs and Patents Act, 1988.

British Library Cataloguing-in-Publication Data

A catalogue record for this book is available from the British Library.

ISBN 1 86126 296 5

Dedication
To Robert, who keeps my chin off the ground and my feet on it; thank you!

Many thanks to the following for generously donating materials: Craft Creations, Hallmark Cards UK, Maple Textiles, Paperchase, G. F. Smith & Son Ltd (Mr Ray Barrell), Tonertex, Dylon International; as well as friends, Sheila Yale, Marlene Cohen, Gargi Chawla, Hilary Jarratt, Kathleen Hodgson, Ann Rutherford, Tom Sawyer, Jan Eaton, Wendy Lawson, and Elaine Thomson and her hands.

Thank you also to Robert Claxton for photographing the cards and steps, and to Steve Tanner who is such a pleasure to work with and makes my creations look wonderful.

Typeface used: Melior

Photography by Steve Tanner and Robert Claxton
Artworks by Annette Findlay
Designed and Typeset by Textype Typesetters, Cambridge
Printed and bound by Leo Paper Products, China

Contents

Introduction

Hand-made greetings cards offer an opportunity to be creative on a small but manageable scale. My own family have always made cards, from the youngest, using hand and foot prints, to the most senior, who makes complicated three-dimensional cut-work creations. We take pleasure in both the activity and in giving an affectionate message.

A personalized card can be used to mark any occasion, perhaps the birth of a child, a Valentine, birthday or an invitation to a landmark party. Many of the cards you make will be kept, even framed, and I have endeavoured to present a variety of styles which I hope will inspire you to develop the ideas further. Generally speaking, cards are not expensive to produce; some are easily made in multiples, while others are suitable for supervised children. Have fun letting your imagination and creative abilities grow – it is surprising how often one card leads to another!

The book is arranged into the four seasons, and features cards to celebrate well-known festivals as well as more general themes. Unless specified, all the cards have a vertical fold, and templates are given to size and in reverse, where necessary, so that when finished they will appear the correct way round. In some cases card dimensions are not specified as the motifs you produce will vary in size. Step-by-step instructions and diagrams make the techniques easy to follow.

Many of the materials can be found at home. It is definitely a bonus if you enjoy collecting, have a sharp eye for tiny objects or are interested in recycling. Get into the habit of keeping an ideas box (or two) into which you pop ribbons, sequins, old greetings cards, stamps and shells.

Enjoy this delightful craft, but take the time to read Chapter 1 as it contains practical advice on achieving the best results, as well as what to do when things go wrong, essential when producing *hand-made* as opposed to *home-made* cards.

A collection of cherished contemporary cards.

THE HISTORY OF GREETING CARDS

The origin of the sending of cards or tokens can be traced back to pagan times. Valentinus, a Roman priest, was beaten and executed for his Christian faith, and although he had no association with lovers, he became their patron saint rather by accident. In Britain, Christian priests looking for a substitute for the fertility rites which took place during the pagan Festival of Lupercalia, celebrated during the Roman occupation, introduced St Valentine as a suitable saints day. It seemed appropriate as his death on 14 February coincided with the eve of the pagan festival marking Spring, when both birds and young men's fancies turned to thoughts of love. Thus the Roman cupid is associated with romance.

Over the years the practice of marking St Valentine's day with expensive gifts and mottos evolved, and by the sixteenth century hand-made cards were sent. These often contained hand-written verses and notes taken from booklets composed by specialist Valentine writers. Sometimes the cards were rather coarse, with humourous vignettes featuring flirtations and infidelities. This fashion for robust comic illustrations and messages has appeared from time to time throughout the history of greetings cards and continues today.

By Victorian times these tokens were hand-made by both men and women, working in secrecy. By using the language of flowers a young man could reveal his desires without offence; forget-me-nots meant constancy and faithfulness, while roses signified true love. The use of daisies indicated innocence, and the lily, purity.

As technology improved, cards became more complex, featuring wonderful three-dimensional motifs, romantic verses, perfumed cushions and silk ribbons. In 1834, beautiful pierced lace-like paper for borders could be made by machine. The cards became even more inventive, some featuring complicated folding (rather like origami) to puzzle the recipient; these often contained a lock of hair or even a ring. Valentine cards were also produced as blanks so that they could contain a personalized message and be hand-embellished.

By the mid-nineteenth century Valentine cards had begun to lose popularity in Britain, overtaken by the Christmas card. Valentines exported to the United States, however, continued to grow in popularity. Christmas cards, rather like Valentines, developed from charms and small tokens used in ancient pre-Christian times to celebrate the festival of Winter Solstice. Later these tokens were given by tradesmen in the form of small calling cards or even calendars, as a subtle form of advertising.

It is generally acknowledged that the first Christmas card was designed by John Calcott Horsley in 1843, when one thousand hand-coloured lithographs about the size of a playing card were commissioned by Sir Henry Cole, who later founded the Victoria and Albert Museum. The illustration featured a Victorian family celebrating Christmas with quantities of food. The scene was contained within a border of branches, and at either side of the card the family's servants were to be seen giving food and warmth to the poor.

The Christmas card was thought to be a passing fad, but manufacturers, quick to realize a business opportunity and following on from the popularity of Valentine cards, produced more the following year. Sometimes the same

designs were used and printed with the appropriate sentiment. Simpler productions were also common, usually featuring an elaborate letterhead together with a seasonal message. Later, with the advent of the Post Office special rates, more elaborate greetings cards became popular. Then as now the themes were of food and family, robins, flowers, snow, mistletoe and holly, as well as those marking the religious significance of the occasion. The illustrations were accompanied by appropriate poems and messages.

The study of these cards provides engrossing material illustrating social history, humour and the lifestyles of our forefathers. During Victorian times, cards received much attention at family gatherings, providing a talking point as well as an opportunity to catch up with long-lost friends; photographs of a family were particularly valued. Many of the cards formed collections and were mounted in albums, particularly by children. They enjoyed scenes in which

unsuspecting senior gentlemen were bombarded by snowballs thrown by waiting children, and similar gentlemen with umbrellas blown inside out walked into pillar boxes.

It is amusing to note that prior to the Penny Post, charges were often made on delivery rather than dispatch, leading to a lot of ill-feeling during a vogue for rather spiteful Valentine cards. A petition to Parliament from an outraged public led to the postal reform. The Penny Post was introduced in 1840 (1845 in the USA) and consisted of a pre-paid letter or envelope on which an adhesive label (a stamp) was attached. The spread of education enabled the working classes to read and write, making good use of postcards and greetings cards as a form of quick communication.

Around the 1860s, birthday anniversaries, rather like Christmas, were seen as a way to expand the greetings card market, and small single cards featuring flowers and foliage became popular. The designs gradually became more complex, folded, with fringes, as well as embossed with flowers and tasselled cords.

Until the early twentieth century greetings cards were mainly produced in Europe and exported to the United States, but during World War One the market grew as new companies were established there. Postcards also became an increasingly useful form of communication between families and friends. Some of these cards contained comic illustrations or featured puns – a breath of fresh air after Victorian prudishness. Interestingly, the vogue for Valentines faded during the early part of the twentieth century, emerging again around the mid-1920s. To fill this gap, alternative anniversaries were sought; New Year greetings were produced and other occasions such as Mother's Day, Easter and Father's Day marketed.

Mother's Day, although linked to the Christian calendar, has other twentieth century influences. It is celebrated in Britain on the fourth Sunday in Lent, but marked in America and Australia on the second Sunday in May. This disparity probably dates back to the American, Anna Jarvis, who, as a tribute to her own mother, campaigned throughout the USA for a special commemorative day for all mothers. Cards featuring flowers as well as gifts of flowers are often given. Father's day is not celebrated in Britain in quite the same way, but its roots may date from the ancient Babylonians. It was adopted as a custom in America around 1910 and endorsed by President Woodrow Wilson in 1924, who chose a rose to signify the occasion.

From the earliest times, famous artists have been commissioned to design greetings cards, and today galleries and museums, together with charities, compete with retailers for this thriving market. Commercially produced cards can be purchased for almost any

occasion, from 'Thinking of You' to 'Sorry', as well as good wishes for weddings, driving tests, new-born babies, landmark birthdays, anniversaries and wishes of sympathy. While St Valentine was pivotal in the development of greetings cards, and although many of the occasions mark a religious event, most have been commercially driven.

I hope that within the pages of this book you will find inspiration to continue the tradition of making cards for special people, and that it will bring you much personal satisfaction as well as encouraging the recipients to start a contemporary collection of cards.

1 Tools, Materials and Techniques

TOOLS OF THE TRADE

Card-making need not be an expensive hobby, however better results will be achieved if the correct tools are used.

Cutting and measuring

- A steel ruler is ideal for measuring and cutting against.
- A craft knife with snap-off blades, or a scalpel (if you are familiar with one), will ensure clean accurate cuts.
- Self-healing cutting mats have a useful printed grid, but you can also use thick cardboard or vinyl tiles as a base for cutting. To avoid accidents, always clear enough working space and check that no other materials are hidden under the piece you are cutting. Work in good light; a tilted anglepoise lamp will avoid shadows.
- Reserve a pair of scissors for cutting paper and card only. Keep a separate pair for cutting fabric; small embroidery scissors are best for intricate shapes, while pinking

TIP:
Orange sticks and tweezers will help with handling small objects when adding glue. Use jam jar lids or the plastic ends from cardboard tubes for mixing paints and glue if you do not have a palette.

shears and deckle scissors both make interesting decorative edges.

◆ Hole punches can be used to cut a variety of shapes from hearts to flowers. Utilize the cut out shapes on gift cards.

◆ A set square is invaluable for measuring accurate corners.

Adhesives

The correct glue will make quick work of card-making.

◆ Spray glue is particularly handy, but needs to be used in a spray booth, which can be created using a cardboard box and an old telephone directory. Place the cardboard box on its side and open the four flaps. Place an open telephone directory inside the box and place the card on it. Spray from a distance of approximately 30cm (12in). Hand-made or recycled paper is very absorbent so will require an extra burst of glue. Use tweezers to remove small items and turn over a page of the directory each time after gluing so you have a clean base for the next project. Be sure to work in a well-ventilated room, and protect furniture and carpets with newspaper as the spray will drift a long way and is difficult to remove.

◆ PVA or rubber-based glues should be used sparingly; when dry the excess can be rubbed off card but not fabric.

◆ An all-purpose clear adhesive sticks metal, plastic and glass and now comes in gel form which does not 'string'.

◆ Double sided sticky tape will ensure good results. Always buy

the type which has a plastic backing. Double sided sticky pads will attach odd shaped materials to many different surfaces.

◆ Fabrics backed with bonding web can be warm ironed on to card as long as the card is over 240gsm (88lb).

◆ Thin strips of masking tape can be used to temporarily hold cards and materials in place while they are being worked on. It has a light tack so if removed carefully will not cause any damage.

Marking

◆ Always work with a sharp pencil – non-stop propelling pencils are handy as they do not need to be sharpened.

◆ Gold and silver pens, coloured felt tip pens and coloured pencils all add to the quality of a card.

◆ Calligraphic felt tip pens come in different sizes and, with practice, give a professional finish to written messages.

◆ A compass will ensure an accurate circle, and coloured pens can be attached to it with masking tape.

CUTTING

Map out the most economical use of card when cutting multiples from a large piece. Either use a set square and rule guidelines, or use the grid of a cutting mat. A sharp knife will prevent woolly edges, and it is better to pass the blade along the edge of a steel rule twice with moderate pressure rather than once with a heavy hand.

FRENCH FOLD (1)

Paper or very light card will need a French fold in order to stand up. First fold the paper horizontally, matching the corners and edges. Run your fingers along the fold.

SCORING

To achieve a neat fold, measure and mark the centre of the card with a pencil dot. Place the edge of the card on a horizontal line and the dot on a vertical line on the cutting mat. Place the steel rule along the vertical line and gently pass the back of the cutting knife along the edge so that only the skin of the card is cut.

FRENCH FOLD (2)

Next, fold vertically, again matching the edges and corners. Run your fingers along the fold.

TRIMMING

Use a set square and ruled pencil guides or a cutting mat grid to neaten the card. Tidy the edges of the card by trimming, after it has been folded.

CREASE

Crease folds on the back of the card to avoid accidentally marking the front. Run the wrong side of a clean, plastic bevelled-edge ruler firmly along the folded edge. Trim as above, if necessary.

MATERIALS
Card and paper

Card and paper manufacturers have responded to the popularity of hand-made paper by producing many interesting textured finishes. Hand-made paper tends to be expensive, but used in small pieces and combined with commercially produced card it will give a classy effect. Look out for (or order from your local art shop) metallic, cloud effect, parchment, corrugated and textured finishes. A wide variety of ready-cut cards is also available in various finishes, with deckle edges, embossed and printed border lines, and envelopes to fit. The double fold cards with shaped apertures are particularly useful.

It is always disappointing when cards refuse to stand up, and this is caused by using card that is too light or thick, or through poor scoring and folding. The best weight of card is at least 200–300gsm (80–110lb), but 240gsm (88lb) will take the heat of an iron without buckling and is robust enough to hold a metal motif. It is always better to make a French fold if using light card or thick paper.

As well as hand-made paper, the range of paper, from tissue to brown, cellophane to giftwrap, is quite wonderful for a creative person. I save used giftwrap and cut out the uncreased areas, sometimes giving it a press with a warm iron. Keep an eye open for motifs that can be cut out and used on cards. Newsprint or butcher's paper is a cheap white paper which is useful as a working surface and can also be decorated and used as giftwrap.

While in transit, delicate cards can be protected in bubblewrap; colourful metallic padded envelopes are also available from stationery shops.

Decorative Materials

This is the section that makes my fingers itch! Almost any material can be used to produce an attractive card. Here are some of the materials that have inspired me, along with others which will give you further ideas for cards.

Good sources of 'stick-on' motifs are dolls' house shops, stationery suppliers of doilies and DIY stores for more unusual ideas, and it is always worth checking out the kits of creative materials sold for children.

All types of paint, from fabric to gouache and poster, have potential for printing and painting, and so, of course, do felt tip pens. Both car and craft spray paints will also work on paper and fabric. Diluted bleach (three parts water to one part bleach) will remove colour and can therefore be used to create patterns on plain card, paper and fabric, while the wide range of découpage sheets provide a quick and easy design. Foils are an exciting new way of adding colour to freehand or stencilled designs by means of a special adhesive.

Save scraps of all types of fabric, from gingham to silk, as well as novelty designs featuring flowers, animals and toys. When combined with glue or stitched with embroidery thread, delightful cards can be created from these scraps. Felt is invaluable as it does not fray and comes in bright jewel

A selection of decorative materials.

Some enticing creative materials.

colours, so children find it easy to use. Recycled giftwrap, greetings cards and magazines will provide you with more images and do not forget to save foil sweetie papers as well.

On the 'glitzy' front, metallic paper, card, sequins and beads evoke parties and Christmas holidays, while nature provides us with fresh flowers as well as leaves and petals which can be dried. A walk along the beach collecting shells and driftwood is sure to inspire new works of art.

Look around haberdashery depart-ments where bags of ribbon off-cuts as well as bags of sweepings (odds and ends of sequins or other craft materials) can sometimes be purchased cheaply. All types of ribbon can be curled over scissors as can narrow strips of paper. Feathers and new types of embroidery threads and lace can also be found in haberdashery departments. Novelty buttons with their shanks filed off are fun, and do not forget that jumble or boot sales are a good source of beads and old jewellery. Like me, once you get started, you will find it hard to stop!

HINTS AND HOW-TO TECHNIQUES

The following pictures demonstrate techniques common to many of the cards featured in the book, together with general tips and information.

◆ CUTTING DOUBLE SIDED STICKY TAPE INTO STRIPS (*LEFT*)

Cut a length of double sided tape and place it on a cutting mat or vinyl tile. Measure and cut 5mm (¼in) widths. Lift the tape carefully using the tip of the knife.

◆ USING BONDING WEB (*LEFT*)

Trace the desired image on to the paper side of the bonding web. Cut out the shape, just outside the drawn line. Place the fabric paper side up and press with a warm iron. Leave to cool before cutting out the image on the drawn line. Peel off the paper backing and attach to the background fabric. Cover with a cloth and press with a warm iron to activate the glue. Please note that the image you trace will appear in reverse on the finished piece. Where appropriate I have provided the templates in reverse so that they will appear the same way round as on the card.

◆ TRANSFERRING DESIGNS FROM TRACING PAPER

Draw the template on to tracing paper. Turn it over and scribble over the drawn line using a soft pencil. With the image the right way round and using a harder (H) pencil, re-draw over the original lines on to card or fabric.

◆ MARKING VERTICAL DOUBLE FOLD CARDS WITH APERTURES

Open the double fold card with the inside facing upwards. Mark a cross in the top left-hand corner. This is the flap that will be folded and stuck down. Mark a cross at the top of the aperture, so that the image will appear the correct way up.

MARKING HORIZONTAL DOUBLE FOLD CARDS WITH APERTURES

After marking a cross in the top left hand corner, make a second cross in the middle of the right-hand side of the aperture. This will be the top of the image.

APPLYING STICKY TAPE TO THE INNER CARD

To attach a motif behind a curved aperture, stick small pieces of double sided tape around the edge and trim the motif 5mm (¼in) larger than the opening. Use long strips for straight cut-outs.

To seal the card, put long strips of tape around the edges of the centre panel, setting in the tape by 2mm (¹⁄₁₆in) on the right-hand edge. This makes a neat fold as the left-hand side is usually cut slightly shorter.

◆ TEARING AGAINST A RULER
Place a metal ruler in the position along which you wish to tear, hold it down with your fingers and firmly pull against the edge. The paper will probably tear more easily along the grain. Hand-made papers which have fibres, for example as silk or plant, are hard to tear accurately and threads will pull out, however this can be used as an artistic feature.

Making a card

◆ Before starting to make a card, check that you have an envelope to fit. The time spent trying to find an envelope of the right size takes all the pleasure out of card-making. Refer to the following section 'Wrappings' if you need a creative solution, or *see* page 93 for a template.

◆ Plan the motif so that it will fit both the card and envelope. When you have selected your materials and assembled the tools you will need, put any not in use to one side. Make sure you have enough space and light in which to work efficiently, or glue will be spilled, cuts made in the wrong place, and materials lost. It is better to trim the card to size and draw in any decorative border lines before mounting the motif. Work with the card folded when pinking or deckle cutting the edges along a lightly drawn pencil guide. Stop cutting just before the scissors reach the tip and re-align the pattern.

◆ When using dark card, use a silver or gold pen to write your message, or cut a folded piece of light-coloured paper to fit and attach it inside the card at the fold with a thin line of glue. A ribbon, cord or tassel will give the card a lavish look.

◆ If glue is dropped in the wrong place, pop a sequin or piece of ribbon on top, or take the drastic step of cutting the motif into pieces to create a mosaic and mount it over a background paper. Try covering the glue with organza or tissue with cut-out areas showing through. You could also start again, cutting the first piece into shapes and attaching them to gift tags or letters. If a motif is seriously wonky, cut it out, including some of the background card and re-mount it. Sometimes the insert may be upside down; do not try to tear it out but cut off the front of the card and re-glue it to a larger piece of card. Draw a border around it or attach some ribbon. Look upon mistakes as creative challenges!

◆ An easy way to produce large quantities of cards for invitations or special occasions is by making colour photocopies of an original card. These can be embellished with pens, glitter and sequins.

◆ When following design instructions, use *either* metric *or* imperial measurements throughout as the two are incompatible.

Wrappings

What can you do when you have created a wonderful card, only to find that no envelope exists to fit it? The answer is to wrap it or to make an envelope – an opportunity for further creativity!

◆ Lay the card diagonally on a sheet of paper and, starting from the bottom, fold the paper as if wrapping a flat parcel. Arrange the folds to finish on the front, where the triangular flap can be secured with a stick-on motif. If you are sending the card through the post you will also need to use sticky tape on the edges.

◆ As an alternative, try placing the card horizontally on the paper and wrapping it, folding the two ends diagonally. Make invisible closures by using double sided sticky tape under the ends and finish with a pretty ribbon.

◆ When making an envelope to a non-standard size, measure the card, adding 3mm (⅛in) on all sides, and draw the shape on to a large sheet of paper. Find the centre of the card and double the distance from that point to the top of the card , adding 1cm (⅜in) for the overlap. Mark this point. Do the same for the bottom and sides (without the extra allowance for the overlap) and mark each point. Rule a diamond shape, joining the four points. Cut out the four 'V' shapes, one at each corner, where the flaps will fold. Glue to close.

◆ I have provided an envelope template on page 93. This will enable you to make envelopes from any type of paper.

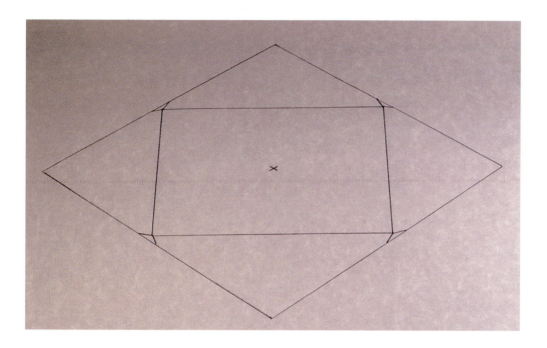

◆ If you do not have the time to make an envelope, and must use one larger than the card, be sure to fold the envelope to fit the card as this will lessen the chance of damage in transit.

◆ Transparent PVC boxes can be purchased to hold delicate 3-D cards, and together with tissue paper and a doily make an impressive presentation. It is also possible to purchase bubblewrap envelopes in bright metallic colours.

2 Spring

Spring is the time of year when our spirits begin to lift after the long Winter. Romantic Valentines, babies and new homes are in our thoughts, and all are featured in this chapter, along with Easter and Mother's Day.

MOTHER'S DAY

The custom of giving flowers on Mother's Day dates from the seventeenth century. As well as floral tributes, mothers are often treated to breakfast in bed or a special lunch cooked by her family. The flowers on this card are fashioned from small beads threaded on to fine wire and wound in circles. The measurements will depend on the size of the beads used.

You will need

- Fine soft wire
- A variety of small glass beads in yellow, red, orange and green
- 21cm x 16cm (8¼in x 6¼in) single fold greetings card
- 8cm (3¼in) square of yellow paper
- Double sided sticky tape
- 25cm (10in) narrow ribbon
- Old scissors

Method

1.   Cut a length of wire 12cm (5in) long. Thread six yellow beads on to the

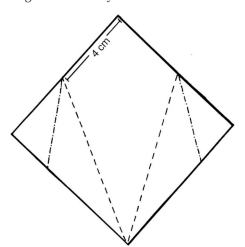

wire and push them towards one end. Form them into a circle and twist that end of the wire around the longer piece to keep the beads in place. Trim off the tail.

2.   Add some orange beads so that they surround the yellow circle. Take the end of the wire and thread it through the gap formed where the yellow beads finish. This will keep the orange beads from slipping. Then add a circle of red beads, finishing in the same way. Finally, thread the green beads to make the stem, twist the wire around the last bead and trim with the scissors.

3.   Make seven flowers altogether, varying the order of colours. Make leaves by threading green beads on wire, pushing them to the centre, forming an oval and twisting the wire to make a double length. Thread more beads to make a stem and finish in the same way as described in (2).

4.   Measure 4cm (1½in) from both sides of one corner of the yellow paper and fold to form a long triangle. Fold the corners back. Place the folded paper on to the card and mark small pencil dots where it will be attached.

5.   Stick one strip of double sided tape on the inside of the paper to hold the flowers in place while you arrange them, plus one strip on the back of the paper. Once you are satisfied with the arrangement, place a second strip of double sided sticky tape over the flowers and close the wrapping paper.

6.   Remove the protective covering from the strip on the back of the bouquet and attach the ribbon before sticking the flowers to the card.

TIP:
Work over a tray or box lid to prevent the beads rolling off the table.

A LITTLE FRAYED AT THE EDGES

With its jewel-like colours, silk always appears to glow. Shot silk is woven from two colours, one from side to side (weft) the other from top to bottom (warp). Here are three ways to achieve quick results using scraps of shot silk, all featuring a frayed background. One card consists of overlapping squares sewn on to a background; the second has a red heart, attached with spray glue and decorated with dimensional fabric paint beads; the third is bonded then decorated with silver pen 'stitches'.

You will need

- Pieces of shot silk, around 9cm x 11cm (3½in x 4¼in)
- Cards cut to fit the silk backgrounds, from 23cm x 16cm (9in x 6¼in) and smaller
- Bonding web
- Spray glue
- Silver pen
- Gold dimensional fabric paint
- Needle and thread
- Scissors

Method

1. Cut a background square and four 3.5cm (1¼in) squares from the shot silk and fray the edges of all the pieces to make a fringe. Arrange the small squares on the backing square of frayed silk, pin, then sew them in place with a small running stitch. Attach the silk to the card with spray glue; make a cut out 'window' to protect the frayed edges and prevent them from getting sticky while spraying the glue.

2. Cut a background square of shot silk and fray the edges. Trace the heart template on page 92 on to bonding web and transfer to the red silk. Cut out the heart. Spray glue the back of the heart, then centre and attach it to the background fabric. Paint little dots of gold dimensional paint around the edge to resemble beads. Leave to dry for about four hours. Use spray glue as described in (1a) to hold the piece in place on the card, and machine-sew using a metallic thread.

3. Cut a 9cm (3in) square of shot silk and fray the edges. Trace out the fleur-de-lys motif on page 93 on to the smooth side of the bonding web. Peel the backing paper away and centre the motif on the silk background before pressing with a warm iron. Mark small 'stitches' around the edge of the motif using a silver pen. Spray glue the silk to hold it in place on the card, then machine-sew with a zig-zag stitch using silver metallic thread.

BE MY VALENTINE

To celebrate St Valentine's Day with a traditional hand-made card, we will create a glitzy padded heart from gold and red organza fabrics. Heart-shaped sequins adorn a gold bow.

You will need

- 10cm (4in) squares of gold fabric and red organza
- 11.5cm (4½in) square of red organza
- 9cm square of card
- 9cm square of wadding
- White and lead pencils
- Needle and thread
- 20cm gold cord
- 4 x heart-shaped sequins
- 27cm x 16.5cm (10½in x 6½in) card
- Pinking shears
- Double sided sticky tape
- Spray glue

Method

1.   Trace the heart template and transfer it to the 9cm square card. Use this first as a template then as the backing for the heart. Draw around the template on to the wadding and cut out the heart shape on the guideline. Using the white pencil so that the line will show, draw around the template again on to the back of the gold and red fabric. Attach the wadding to the card heart with a piece of double sided tape

2.   Leaving a seam allowance of approximately 7mm (¼in), cut out the fabric hearts. Make one small snip into the seam allowance of the hearts, just where the top curves form a 'V' shape, but do not cut the guideline. Starting from the 'V' snip, sew a small running stitch just inside the cut edge of the gold and red hearts. Draw up the thread of the gold heart and insert the card, wadding side down. Manipulate with your fingers so that the stitches do not show on the front, then tie off the ends. Repeat with the red heart. Trim the ends and hold them taut with a small piece of double sided sticky tape.

3.   Tie the gold cord into a bow, sew it on to the heart and glue the gold sequins to the ends.

4.   Centre the organza on the front of the card and mark its position with tiny dots. To attach it to the card, use a cut out 'window' to mask the card so that only a small area is sticky, and spray glue. Attach double sided sticky tape to the back of the heart and glue it into place.

SPINNING

This is a very quick and simple card, but one with impact, made using tissue paper in pale versions of the three primary colours: blue, red and yellow. Random triangles have been cut at each corner of a square through all three layers of tissue paper. The squares have been rotated so that areas of the original tissues show and new colours appear on the overlaps. The luminous effect is enhanced by the beautiful mulberry paper background.

You will need

- ◆ 23cm x 18cm (9in x 7in) single fold card
- ◆ Mulberry paper torn to 10cm x 12cm (4in x 4¾in)
- ◆ Small pieces of turquoise, pink and lemon tissue paper
- ◆ Spray glue
- ◆ Craft knife
- ◆ Steel rule
- ◆ Felt tip pen
- ◆ Stationer's dots
- ◆ Card

Method

1.   Tear the mulberry paper to size. Noting the shiny side of the tissue paper, cut three 6cm (2½in) squares, one of each colour. Using a sharp craft knife cut 1.5cm (½in) triangles in each corner, varying the angles; they should appear to chase each other around. Centre the mulberry paper and the first square and mark their position with a dot. Spray glue the mulberry paper and the three squares on the wrong side, arrange them so that part of all the colours shows through the cut triangles and attach. Cover with a piece of clean paper and smooth flat. Colour white stationer's dots with a felt tip pen to match one of the colours of the tissue paper and attach them in a line as a border at the top and bottom of the card.

2.   Transfer the diamond-shaped template on page 93 to the card. Cut it out and score on the right side to make a triangle. Trace and cut out the smaller triangle template then cut three tracing paper shapes. Arrange them so that the colours overlap and, taking note of their positions, spray glue the back of the triangles before sticking them into place on the card. By repeating the tissue triangles on the reverse you could make a double sided card.

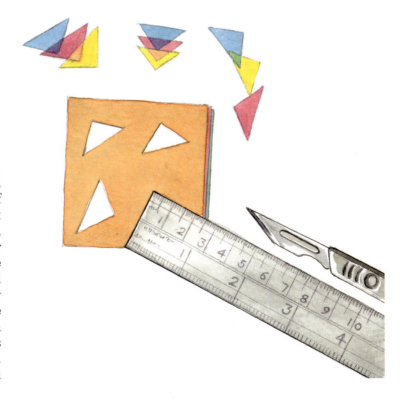

CHERUBS FOR A BABY

This Victorian cherub card could be sent to greet a new-born baby. The cherub is cut from reproduction Victorian scraps mounted over a tracing paper window which is attached to the card from the reverse. One side of the double fold card is cut off so that light will show through, and this off-cut can be used for gift tags or another project.

You will need

- A sheet of Victorian scraps
- Piece of good quality tracing paper cut to 13cm x 16cm (5in x 6¼in)
- 13cm x 16cm (5in x 6¼in) double fold card with a circular aperture
- 3 x ribbon flowers
- Double sided sticky tape
- Spray glue
- Clear adhesive
- Scissors

Method

1.   Cut out the cherub from the sheet of scraps and trim neatly. Cut off the right-hand side of the double fold card.

2.   Cut four 3mm (⅛in) strips of double sided sticky tape and attach them to the edges of the inside front of the card. Place the tracing paper over the top and gently press the edges, starting at the fold towards the edge, first top then bottom.

3.   Apply spray glue to the back of the cherub and attach it to the front of the card. Glue three ribbon flowers to the border.

4.   The two gift tags were made from the off-cut card. One has stick-on flowers attached, the other a cherub and border cut from a paper doily.

WELCOME TO YOUR NEW HOME

Fun to make and sure to raise a smile from the new residents, this welcome card is a collage of magazine pictures of houses. Collect pictures of roofs, windows, front doors, brickwork and plants. The message could be: 'Hope your new home comes together soon!'

You will need

◆ 23cm x 18cm (9in x 7in) single fold card
◆ Old magazines
◆ Paper scissors
◆ Spray glue

Method

1.   Tear out a good selection of pictures from old magazines, varying the sizes of the roofs, windows and doors. Select plenty of the appropriate details so there are enough to choose from. Cut out the shapes and try various arrangements, gradually building a 'crazy' house until you are satisfied with the plan.

2.   Make a few light pencil guidelines to show where the various pieces fit, and note the overlaps and which pieces should be stuck on first.

3.   Spray glue all the pieces on the reverse side. Arrange the house on the card, cover with a clean sheet of paper and smooth the collage flat.

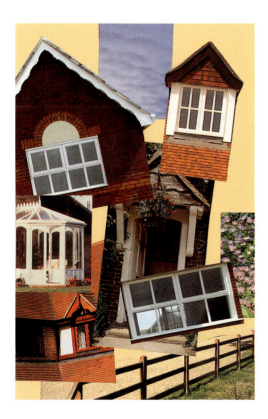

PAPER PATCHWORK STAR

This card is covered with no-sew patchwork made from recycled coloured writing paper in four gentle, pastel colours. Choose a lighter or brighter colour for the triangles marked 'A' on the block design as this will make the star motif stand out from the background. Before gluing the design down, spend some time 'playing' with the shapes and colours.

You will need

- 12cm x 24cm (5in x 9½in) piece of card with a scored centre fold
- 4 x sheets of recycled coloured paper, two with a darker contrast
- Spray glue
- Sharp craft knife

Method

1. Cut a 3cm (1¼in) wide strip from each piece of coloured paper. Cut four 3cm (1¼in) squares from the colours to be used for the star and background, and then cut them diagonally to make triangles. Cut four squares of the same size from the background colour for the corners. Cut two squares from each of the centre colours and divide them diagonally.

2. Copy the grid on page 93 and lightly transfer it to the card using a fine pencil. Mark the star triangles with an 'A'. Mask the left half of the card and cover the grid with spray glue.

3. Arrange the star shape on the triangles marked 'A'. Then fill in the outside shapes, and finally the centre. Cover with a piece of clean paper and smooth flat. Neaten the edges by trimming them with a steel rule and craft knife.

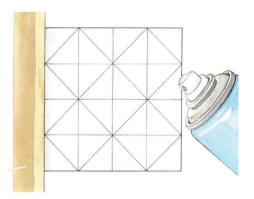

4. The two bow-tie gift tags consist of squares arranged diagonally with an overlapping 'knot'. Cut three squares of one colour and two of a contrast colour. Spray glue the squares on the back and attach two of each colour in a checkerboard arrangement, then add the final square so that each corner touches a diagonal join.

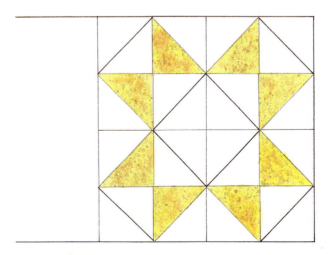

SPRING CHICKEN

A tongue-in-cheek card sure to bring a smile to everyone's face at Easter. A combination of scraps of fabric and stitch, feathers and corrugated card make a little work of art, which, if framed, could become a gift.

You will need

- ◆ 30cm x 20cm (12in x 8in) corrugated card
- ◆ 3 x small pieces of 'country' fabric – 10cm x 8cm (4in x 3in)
- ◆ Small piece of black-and-white-striped fabric
- ◆ Tiny piece of red felt
- ◆ 15cm x 20cm (6in x 8in) background fabric
- ◆ A few co-ordinated feathers
- ◆ Bonding web
- ◆ Black and co-ordinating *coton à broder* thread no. 16
- ◆ Tiny button for chicken's eye
- ◆ 4 x pearl buttons
- ◆ Scissors

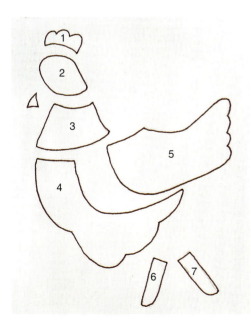

Method

1. Trace out seven chicken templates on page 92 on to bonding web. Move the paper each time to separate the templates. Cut out, just outside the drawn line. Place the 'chickens' paper side up and press with a warm iron. Leave to cool then cut out on the drawn line. Peel off the protective paper and arrange all the pieces on the background fabric. Cover with a cloth and press. Leave to cool.

2. The stitches should be visible, so use *coton à broder* embroidery thread to sew straight appliqué stitches around the outside of the chicken. Add more stitch detail if you wish.

3. Turn back 1cm (½in) of the background fabric all around the edge and sew it down with a visible running stitch. Using black thread, backstitch the claw details. Sew on the eye button.

4. Centre the piece on the front of the card and mark each corner with a pencil dot, then hold it in place with a small dab of glue. Place the opened card on a pad of felt or newspaper, put the buttons in the corners and push a thick needle through to make pilot holes where the buttons will be fixed. Sew the buttons through these holes, finishing with a knot and a dab of glue to secure them. Glue the feathers into place.

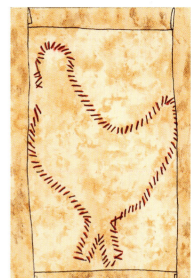

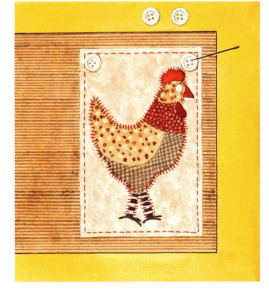

3 Summer

We all look forward to languid Summer days; a time for travelling, relaxing on holiday, entertaining friends or tending our gardens. Bright colours together with images of landscapes and sea shores will inspire you with new ideas.

ON THE SEA SHORE

This card will evoke memories of Summer holidays through the use of miniature sea shells. It is hard to resist collecting shells when strolling along the beach or sitting on the sand, and these shells have been varnished to resemble their colours when wet. The tiny, delicate and perfect shapes found in my collection make a beautiful birthday or general purpose card.

You will need

◆ 12 x similar size tiny sea shells
◆ Tissue paper in two colours
◆ Clear adhesive
◆ 23cm x 18cm (9in x 7in) single fold card
◆ Spray varnish
◆ Tweezers
◆ Tracing paper
◆ Craft knife

Method

1.   Work in a well-ventilated room. Select the shells, lay them on a sheet of newspaper to protect the surrounding area from drifting varnish, or use a spray booth, and spray them with varnish and leave to dry. Apply a second coat if necessary. While the shells are drying, cut six small, roughly square pieces of tissue paper from each colour.

2.   To produce the wave edge at the top and bottom of the card, trace the template. Open the card flat and lightly transfer the wave, first to the top left-hand side, then to the right, following the curved line. Repeat for the bottom edges. Carefully cut out using scissors or a craft knife. Leave a little 'foot' in the centre to enable the card to stand.

3.   Spray glue the back of the tissue paper squares and apply to the right-hand side of the card, overlapping the edges. Cover with a clean sheet of paper and smooth flat. Remove the paper and glue the tiny shells in place using a clear adhesive. Hold the shells with tweezers so that they do not roll over. Leave to dry.

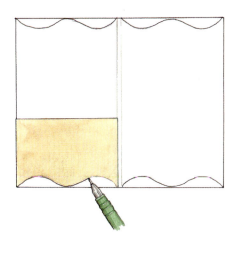

TIP:
If the card is to be posted, use a piece of bubblewrap to protect the shells.

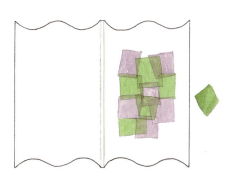

TRAVELLING LIGHT

Stamps are fascinating little works of art and often arrive on postcards from exotic places. Here I have made a collage from small stamps and attached them to a suitcase-shaped card – a '*Bon Voyage*' message, perhaps!

You will need

- 14.5cm x 20cm (6in x 8in) tan-coloured horizontal fold card
- Two strips of 1cm x 10cm (¼in x 4in) tan card
- 14.5cm x 10cm (6in x 4in) white paper
- A quantity of small, brightly coloured stamps
- Spray glue
- Craft knife
- Steel rule

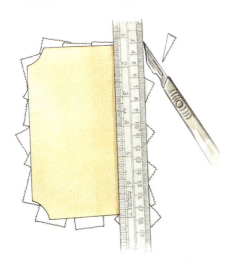

Method

1. To remove stamps from envelopes, soak them in cold water for 15 minutes, then leave them to dry, face-down, on kitchen paper.

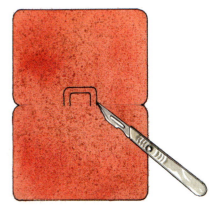

2. Enlarge the suitcase front (dotted) line template by 240 per cent on to the white paper. Cut out the curved corners.

3. When the stamps are dry, place them face-down on a slightly sticky page of the phone book in your spray booth to prevent them blowing about, and apply spray glue. When handling the stamps, hold them on the tip of a craft knife or use tweezers. Cover the white paper with the stamps, starting from the centre and overlapping their edges, arranging them so that no background can be seen. Cover with a sheet of clean paper and smooth flat. Trim any stamps to fit.

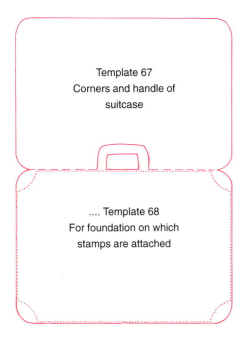

Template 67
Corners and handle of
suitcase

.... Template 68
For foundation on which
stamps are attached

4. Trim the corners of the suitcase card and cut the handle out of the reverse side. Lift the handle up. Using spray glue, apply the stamp collage to the front.

SUMMER SAILS

Bright sails racing along on silver-topped waves are a pleasure to watch while sitting comfortably on the beach. Here, abstract shapes have been used to give surprisingly realistic effects.

You will need

- 32cm x 14cm (12½in x 5½in) turquoise card
- 11.5cm x 13.5cm (4½in x 5¼in) pale green card or 23cm x 9cm (9in x 3½in) horizontal fold card
- A variety of different textured papers to represent sea and sails,
- including tissue paper in two colours
- Magazines or holiday brochures
- Spray glue
- Scissors
- Craft knife

Method

1. Lay out the various textured papers so that the effect of the tissue paper overlaps can be seen. Cut two rectangles of approximately 4cm x 7.5cm (1½in x 3in), one of 3cm x 7.5cm (1¼in x 3in) and one of 2.5cm x 7.5cm (1in x 3in). Divide them diagonally to make the sail shapes. Cut the shiny paper into a wave shape and trim to 2.5cm x 14cm (1in x 5½in). Cut the cloud-patterned paper and the darker grey paper to the same size.

2. Arrange the shapes on the green card, overlapping the waves and the sails. Take note of their positions, then remove and spray glue the backs of all the pieces. Attach the red and blue sails first, placing the line of shiny waves over them. Next add the tissue paper sails, followed by the two sets of waves.

3. Cut tiny triangles for the pennant flags and attach these to the card. Neaten the edges of the card by cutting with a sharp craft knife, then attach the sailing scene to the turquoise card.

4. For the second card, I have followed the technique above but used a horizontal fold card.

TIP:
Good sources of textured patterns are magazine advertisements and holiday catalogues.

PRESSED FLOWER PETALS

Flowers, leaves and petals gathered when the dew has dried can be easily pressed by placing them between the pages of an old telephone directory or by using a simple flower press. Even the most modest leaf will come into its own when applied to an interesting hand-made paper background. Here are some different approaches to using pressed petals.

You will need

- Selection of dried leaves and petals, including two clover leaves
- Hand-made or interesting textured paper
- 10cm x 15cm (4in x 6in) card (clover)
- 15cm x 20cm (6in x 8in) double fold card with oval aperture
- Small piece of patterned paper for the vase
- Small piece of tracing paper
- PVA glue
- Pair of tweezers
- Orange stick
- Spray glue
- Tracing paper
- Scissors

Method

FOUR-LEAVED CLOVER

1.   Cut a small piece of the hand-made paper – 6.5cm x 8cm (2½in x 3¼in). Remove the leaves from the two clovers and re-assemble and glue as shown. Using spray glue, attach the 'four-leaved clover' to the top left-hand side of the 10cm x 15cm (4in x 6in) card.

Using a selection of the petals, apply six flower heads down the right-hand side of the card, and stick the petals in a horizontal row. Cover with a piece of clean paper and smooth flat.

VASE ARRANGEMENT

1.   Place the hand-made paper under the oval aperture of the card and lightly draw the outline using a fine pencil. Trace the vase shape template and transfer it to the back of the patterned paper. Cut out and lightly draw the top edge of the vase in place as a guideline. Start arranging the top outer leaves and larger flowers in position. Glue them into place then attach the vase. Fill in with an arrangement of smaller flowers. Cover with a piece of clean paper and smooth over the flowers. The paper background may have shrunk, so carefully erase the oval guideline. Remembering to mark the fold down side and top of the double fold card with an 'X', insert the flower arrangement and attach as shown on page 16.

The smaller cards are made in the same manner.

TIP:

When working with delicate petals, it is best to pick them up and hold them with a pair of tweezers, and to dab tiny spots of glue using the tip of an orange or cocktail stick.

LIGHTHOUSE

No longer manned, lighthouses now provide interesting holiday accommodation and remain a stirring reminder of the past as we see them on holiday coastline walks. The effect of the lighthouse standing on a clifftop is achieved here by attaching it to the card with sticky pads.

You will need

- ◆ double fold card with aperture 9.5cm x 15cm (3¾in x 6in)
- ◆ 10cm x 15cm (4in x 6in) piece of white card
- ◆ 4 x double sided sticky pads
- ◆ Felt tip pens in red, black and blue
- ◆ Blue coloured pencil
- ◆ 3cm (1¼in) square piece of silver paper
- ◆ Textured white cartridge paper slightly larger than the aperture
- ◆ Small piece of tracing paper
- ◆ Craft knife or sharp scissors

Method

1.   Trace the lighthouse template, enlarge it by 110 per cent and transfer the design on to the white card.

2.   Draw the balcony railings using a black felt tip pen. Cut the silver paper to fit and glue into place. Decorate the tower with the red chequerboard pattern using a felt tip pen. Fill in the black rocky base of the tower with the black pen. Holding the blue pencil horizontally, colour the sky, using darker shading at the top and becoming lighter. Work over the darker area several times rather than using pressure to achieve the shade. Fill in the blue sea area using the blue felt tip pen.

3.   Attach the background to the wrong side of the aperture, remembering to mark the left-hand flap with an 'X'. Glue the flap into place.

4.   Finally, trim the double sided sticky pads before fixing them to the back of the lighthouse and rocks. Peel off the outer covering and press on to the sky/sea background.

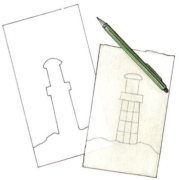

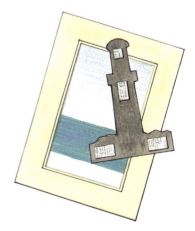

POPPYFIELD

This card serves as a reminder of Summer cornfields and poppies, and uses tiny pieces of chopped silk to recreate a landscape resembling the thick paintstrokes of Vincent Van Gogh.

You will need

- ◆ 15cm x 20cm (6in x 8in) double fold horizontal aperture card
- ◆ 20cm x 25cm (8in x 10in) square of white fabric, ready washed and pressed
- ◆ Blue and yellow fabric paints
- ◆ Small sponge
- ◆ 2 x small jam jar lids
- ◆ Paintbrush
- ◆ Scraps of silk in blues, greens, yellows and reds
- ◆ 11cm x 30cm (4½in x 12in) bonding web
- ◆ White newsprint or an old sheet
- ◆ Scissors

Method

1.   Draw a guideline shape slightly larger than the card aperture. Fold the newsprint or old sheet to make a pad and tape the corners of the white fabric to it.

2.   Pour some yellow and blue paint into each of the jam jar lids, adding a little water if necessary. Starting with the blue sky area, sponge paint on to the fabric with light quick movements, overlapping the edges of the guideline. Next add the yellow cornfield, then mix together the blue and yellow paint to make green and sponge in the trees and shrubs. Put to one side to dry. Cover with a cloth and press with a hot iron to set the paint.

3.   Chop the silk into tiny pieces, keeping the colours separate. Cut the bonding web in half. Peel the paper from one half and snip the web into tiny pieces. Place the other half over the painted area with the paper side uppermost. Press with a hot iron, and when cool peel off the paper covering.

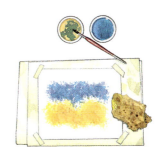

4.   Create texture by scattering the pieces of silk 'confetti' on to the prepared background in a landscape arrangement. Add the pieces of bonding web. Cover with the bonding web to protect the base of the iron and press.

5.   Remember to mark the side of the card to be folded and glued down and the 'top' of the inside of the aperture with a cross. Attach double sided sticky tape to the inside of the card.

6.   Place the picture beneath the aperture and mark a pencil dot register in each corner. Rule a 5mm (½in) cutting line outside the dots on all sides and cut out. Mount the picture (*see* page 16) and close the card.

YOU ARE MY SUNSHINE

Sunshine is welcome at any time of year, and in this card the sun is cut from lightweight brass. Mounted on a sticky pad over a disk of gold card, the curved rays have been slightly bent towards the card so that they do not catch on anything. Thin metal is available from craft and modelmaking shops.

You will need

- 23cm x 18cm (9in x 7in) single fold card
- 18cm (7in) square piece of gold paper
- 13cm (5in) square piece of brass sheet
- 13cm (5in) square card for template
- Sharp (H) pencil
- Compass
- Permanent ink pen
- Double sided sticky tape
- Spray glue
- Sticky pad
- Tracing paper
- Scissors or craft knife

METHOD

1.   Enlarge the sun template by 130 per cent and transfer it on to the template card. Cut out and hold it in place on the back of the tin with a piece of double sided sticky tape. Draw around the outside of the sun's rays. Remove the template and cut out, using a craft knife or scissors. Slightly bend the tips of the sun's rays over towards the back.

2.   Using a compass, draw two circles of 10.5cm (4⅛in) and 4cm (1½in) diameter on the back of the gold paper and cut out. Centre the larger circle on the single fold card and mark with a dot, then spray glue on the back and stick it into place. Transfer the sun's features to the smaller circle using a permanent ink pen then spray glue it to the metal sun. Attach a sticky pad to the back of the sun and stick it in place over the gold disc.

LA MER

Unusual results are achieved here, all featuring a sea theme, by using foil with a special embossing adhesive. This is another technique of interest to children, as all kinds of items, including fabric, can be decorated. The pressure-sensitive adhesive is left to dry before gently touching it with the foil which transfers instantly.

You will need

- 1 x bottle of pressure-sensitive adhesive
- Small pieces of gold, marble and rainbow foils
- Small piece of hand-made paper
- Small piece of crinkle cellophane
- Small scallop shell
- 2 pieces of card, 11cm x 7.5cm (4½in x 3in) and 8cm (3in) square
- Single fold cards
- Sharp (H) pencil
- Double sided sticky tape
- Sewing machine with metallic thread
- Spray glue
- Tracing paper
- Sticky pad
- Scissors or craft knife

Method

1. Trace the fish template and transfer it, using a sharp pencil, to a

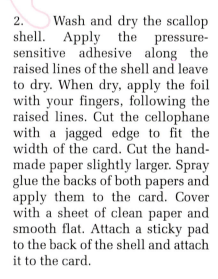

small piece of card. Cover the lines with the pressure-sensitive adhesive and leave to dry. This could take up to four hours. Place the rainbow foil, colour side up, on to the fish shape. Press gently, tracing the outline with your fingers, lifting the foil as it transfers to the adhesive. Attach the fish card to a horizontal fold card using a couple of pieces of double sided sticky tape in the centre of the back. Using a metallic thread on the sewing machine, sew around the edge of the fish card. Tie the ends of the thread off at the back and use a dot of glue to hold them in place. Finish with some spots of adhesive and foil to make bubbles and corner trims.

2. Wash and dry the scallop shell. Apply the pressure-sensitive adhesive along the raised lines of the shell and leave to dry. When dry, apply the foil with your fingers, following the raised lines. Cut the cellophane with a jagged edge to fit the width of the card. Cut the hand-made paper slightly larger. Spray glue the backs of both papers and apply them to the card. Cover with a sheet of clean paper and smooth flat. Attach a sticky pad to the back of the shell and attach it to the card.

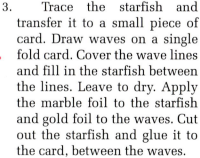

3. Trace the starfish and transfer it to a small piece of card. Draw waves on a single fold card. Cover the wave lines and fill in the starfish between the lines. Leave to dry. Apply the marble foil to the starfish and gold foil to the waves. Cut out the starfish and glue it to the card, between the waves.

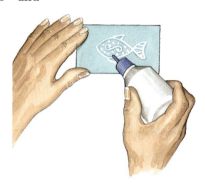

4 Autumn

Hazy Autumn days, when sunsets are at their best, herald those first crisp mornings as leaves begin to fall and our lives pick up speed again after the lazy days of Summer. In this chapter our thoughts turn to harvest festivals and celebrations such as Hallowe'en.

DIAMONDS AND STARS

Felt is a most accommodating fabric; it has no grain, does not fray and comes in wonderful bright colours. Here, simple star, circle and diamond shapes have been cut from the centres of squares, then exchanged.

You will need

- Small squares of felt at least 6cm (2½in) in four colours, and one 14cm (5½in) square in a contrasting colour
- 6cm x 20cm (2½in x 8in) bonding web
- 16cm x 32cm (6¼in x 12½in) and 9cm x 18cm (3½in x 7in) double fold cards
- Cotton fabric backing for circles
- Sharp craft knife
- Pinking shears
- Steel ruler
- Double sided sticky tape

Method

1.   Using a sharp pencil, trace two sets of star and diamond template squares on to the smooth side of the bonding web. Cut them out, just outside the drawn line, and press them on to the appropriate colour felt using a warm iron.

2.   Using pinking shears, cut around each square following the drawn lines. Cut out the star and diamond motifs using a sharp craft knife held against the edge of a steel ruler.

3.   Peel off the backing paper and arrange the squares on to the larger piece of felt, exchanging the motifs. Protect the squares with a pressing cloth and use a warm iron to set them in place.

4.   Centre the motifs and mark their position with a couple of pencil dots, then attach to the card with double sided sticky tape.

5.   The small cards are made by drawing two pairs of circles on to bonding web and exchanging them, following the technique above but attaching them to a backing circle.

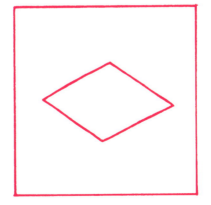

TEDDY BEARS' PICNIC INVITATION

This is an invitation for teddy bears, together with their owners, to come to an Autumn picnic! The teddy bear theme could be continued with a teddy-shaped Birthday cake, sandwiches cut with a teddy biscuit cutter, and teddy tablewear and goodie bags. These cards are easy and quick to make and are an ideal project for children.

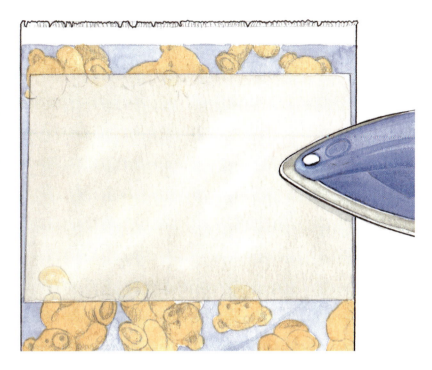

You will need

- 25cm x 114cm (9¾in x 42in) teddy bear fabric
- Bonding web
- 240gsm (88lb) cards
- Narrow ribbon
- Coloured paper
- Brown paper bags
- Paper napkins
- Scissors

Method

1. Apply the bonding web to the reverse of the fabric by pressing with a warm iron. Leave to cool.

2. Carefully cut out the teddy motifs and attach them to the cards by pressing with a warm iron. Leave to cool. Add balloons with ribbons.

3. The motifs can also be applied to table napkins, goodie bags, as well as clothing.

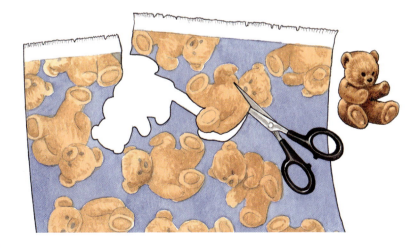

TIP:
When using bonding web, always protect your ironing board cover with a spare piece of fabric or baking parchment.

HARVEST TIME AND THANKSGIVING

Both of these occasions mark the celebration of gathering the harvest, when families meet to enjoy the tradition of a Thanksgiving meal. In this card I have used slices of dried orange to symbolize anniversaries; we are used to seeing dried flowers, but fruit and vegetables also make decorative cards and pictures.

You will need

- ◆ One small firm orange
- ◆ 31cm x 11cm (12in x 4¼in) card with a horizontal fold
- ◆ 19cm x 11cm (7½in x 4¼in) card
- ◆ Coloured raffia
- ◆ Green and orange hand-made paper
- ◆ Paper napkin with a Thanksgiving theme
- ◆ Green paper (two tones)
- ◆ Steel ruler
- ◆ Spray glue
- ◆ Needle and thread
- ◆ Craft knife and scissors

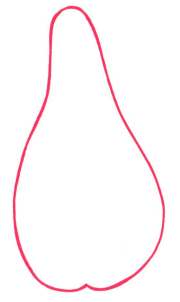

Method

1.   Slice the orange very thinly, around 3mm (⅛in). Place the slices on a baking sheet and bake them in the oven overnight on the lowest setting (your house will smell wonderful!). Tear the hand-made paper, holding it firmly against the edge of a steel ruler. The paper may not tear very easily, depending on the type, so keep an open mind as to the finished shape! Spray glue the hand-made paper, giving it a second blast as it tends to be very absorbent. Attach it to the main card. Make a bow from the coloured raffia, and sew through the dried orange, the raffia bow and the card, securing the threads at the back with a knot and a dab of glue.

2.   Trace the apple and pear templates and transfer each to the back of one of the green papers. Cut out the shapes and remove the border from the napkin. Spray glue the border, as well as the apple and pear and attach them to the second card. Sew through the centre of the orange, securing the thread at the back with a knot and a dab of glue.

3.   Make the gift tag using the same technique. Use ring-binder reinforcing washers coloured with a felt tip pen and add a raffia tie. Add a bead, held in place with a knot.

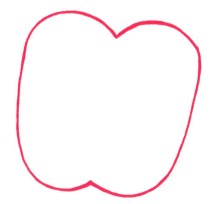

JEWISH NEW YEAR

Two versions of the distinctive skyline of Jerusalem bring messages of peace and good wishes to greet the New Year. For the first card I have used bronze glitter fabric paint on white organza; the second is made from painted silk with the colours chosen to evoke the reflections of sunrise or sunset on the city.

You will need

GLITTER PAINT

- 23cm x 16cm (9in x 6½in) card with a horizontal fold
- White organza, at least 28cm (11¼in) square
- Bronze glitter fabric paint
- Embroidery or old picture frame

PAINTED SILK CARD

- 33cm x 15cm (13in x 6in) card
- Washed white Haboutai silk, at least 28cm (11¼in) square
- Gold gutta
- Turquoise, blue, cherry, red and apricot silk paints
- 2 or 3 x paintbrushes, from sizes 00 to 9
- Pot of water

- Kitchen paper
- Sharp pencil
- Masking tape
- Scissors
- Spray glue

Method

GLITTER PAINT CARD

1.   Trace the template on page 92 on to a sheet of paper, holding it in place on the worktop with pieces of masking tape. Centre and tape the organza over the drawing, keeping the fabric taut. Trace the drawing on to the material. Attach the prepared design to a frame, keeping the fabric taut and using

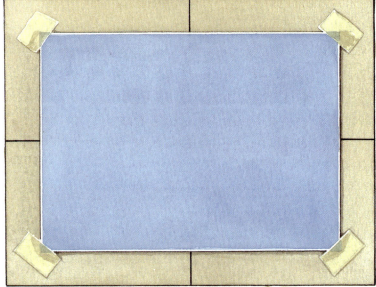

TIP:

It is easier to work on a frame if all sides of the fabric are supported. If you do not have a frame to fit, use a piece of fabric larger than the design you are painting.

masking tape on all sides. Keep a piece of kitchen paper handy to wipe any blobs from the nozzle of the paint dispenser. Following the manufacturer's instructions and starting at the centre of the picture, cover the lines with glitter paint. Leave to dry, then cut out around the outside of the oval shape.

TIP 2:

It is always difficult to know how a colour will appear when dry, so draw up a grid of 2.5cm (1in) squares, with extra for when you buy more paint. Apply gutta, allow it to set, then paint and label each square. Paints can of course be mixed, but always use a palette or a saucer.

TIP 1:

Silk is very absorbent, so it is necessary to use gutta lines to stop the colours running. Drying time can be speeded up by the use of a hairdryer, but do not attempt to start painting until the gutta is dry.

2.   Trace the oval shape on to a piece of paper or card and use it as a mask. Centre the front of the card over the mask and hold in place with masking tape. Spray glue then carefully remove the card from the mask. Attach the image on to the oval glued area (remembering to place it the right side up) and cover with a sheet of white paper. Smooth to flatten.

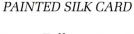
PAINTED SILK CARD

1.   Follow step 1a then attach the silk to a frame with masking tape. Keeping a piece of kitchen paper in one hand to wipe off the first blob from the nozzle, apply the gold gutta to the lines of the design. Leave to dry. Hold the piece up to the light and double check that there are no breaks in the gutta line which the colours can flow through. Add more gutta if necessary.

Shake the paints, then open them well away from the prepared piece as the tiny bubbles send spray a surprisingly long way. Mix a medium paintbrush-full of red paint with water and apply around the skyline. Using the large paintbrush, immediately add the blue so that the colours blend. Washing the paintbrush between applications, paint the turquoise domes with the medium brush, followed by the buildings. Finally, paint the windows with a small brush. Leave to dry, then cover with a cloth and press.

2.   If the pieces are to be mounted in window cards, follow the instructions on page 16. However, to keep the brightness of the colours, I have cut an oval of white card as a backing for the picture and then put this on to a darker card.

TIP 3:

If a serious paint run spoils a picture, all is not lost. Do not throw it away, but cut it into small squares, strips or triangles. Spray glue these images on the back, lay them on thin card and turn them into gift tags!

HALLOWE'EN

The excitement of a Hallowe'en party is captured in this invitation. Hallowe'en is the night when children, heavily disguised as witches and ghouls, demand 'trick or treat!' Have your treats ready for their arrival!

You will need

- A collection of thin twigs, and one thicker twig for the broom handle
- Glitter or metallic spray
- 23cm x 18cm (9in x 7in) single fold card
- Silver yarn
- Small piece of yellow card
- Small adhesive stars
- Silver felt tip pen
- Plastic ruler
- Double sided sticky tape
- Clear adhesive
- Scissors or craft knife

Method

1. Trim the thin twigs to about 6cm (2¼in) and the thicker twig to 8cm (3in). Wrap the smaller twigs around the end of the 'broom handle' and bind with silver yarn, securing the ends with a knot at the back.

2. Following the instructions on the can and using a spray booth, spray the glitter over the broom in short bursts, leaving to dry between each coat.

3. Trace the moon shape and transfer it to the reverse of the yellow card.

4. To draw a border, lightly rule two guidelines in pencil at diagonal sides of the card. Draw over the guidelines with the silver felt tip, leaving each line to dry before starting the next. This only takes a few seconds. To avoid smudging the silver ink, use a ruler with a bevelled edge, reverse side up.

5. Attach the moon using double sided sticky tape, and glue the broom in place using clear adhesive. Arrange and attach some stars around the design and, finally, spray a light dusting of glitter over the card.

AUTUMN LEAVES

Simple printing is an excellent technique for cards, and one which children particularly enjoy. I have used leaves, both as a print and as a stencil outline, but there are many other objects around the home that could be used to equally good effect; experiment with finger prints, shaped erasers, corks and vegetables. Leaves are always readily available, but do get into the habit of pressing specimens in telephone directories all year round. Also, try using several types of paper and be prepared to find creative uses for the odd mishap!

You will need

◆ Pots of red, green and yellow
acrylic or fabric paint
◆ 3 x saucers and spoons
◆ Pot of water
◆ Paintbrush, approximately size 8
◆ Several types of paper
◆ Kitchen paper
◆ A variety of leaves with pronounced veins and outlines
◆ Sheet of newsprint to protect working surfaces
◆ Card in various colours and sizes
◆ Brown paper
◆ Masking tape

Method

1.   Read the instructions on the paint pots before pouring the individual colours into their own saucer. If necessary, add a little red to the yellow to give it a richer tone and a little green to the red if it is too bright.

2.   Lay out the papers ready for printing and hold them in place with a piece of masking tape.

3.   Try a practice leaf first. Place it, face-down, on a piece of kitchen paper and, using a paintbrush, coat it with

TIP:
Prepare the kitchen paper by tearing along the perforations and placing it in a pile, ready to use.

paint. Put the leaf on to the paper, paint side down, cover with a piece of clean kitchen paper and press down using fingers or a roller. Carefully lift the leaf to avoid smudging. The print will vary according to the type of leaf, its age and the absorbency of the paper used. Print the first leaf on all the pieces of paper and leave to dry. Next print another leaf in a contrast colour, building up a pattern. Finally, print using the last colour and leave to dry.

4.   With any leftover paint, use some leaves as stencils. Place them on the paper and gently sponge around them so that a reverse silhouette remains.

5.   Cut out the leaf arrangements and attach to cards of different colours and sizes.

6.   To make the wrapping paper, lightly spray glue on to one side of the leaves and position them on brown paper. Use a combination of aerosol paint and light sponging.

5 Winter

The excitement of Christmas holiday celebrations dominate this season. This is a time for families and friends to meet and take part in familiar traditions, and an opportunity to take pleasure in our warm, snug homes, looking out at frosty starlit nights.

THE HOLLY AND THE IVY

Here is a way to speed up the production of hand-made cards when a great many are required, for example Christmas cards or party invitations. Technology comes to our aid, as the holly and ivy leaves are simply scanned into a computer then printed in multiples. The results are so impressive you can fool your friends into believing you have propagated a holly and ivy hybrid in your garden! To follow are a variety of ways in which the motif can be made up incorporating several background papers and different shaped cards.

You will need

◆ One holly and one ivy leaf
◆ Computer, flat-bed scanner and colour printer
◆ Various types of card, colour co-ordinated with a variety of tissue, recycled and hand-made papers
◆ Small piece of cellophane
◆ Correcting pen
◆ Spray glue
◆ Steel rule
◆ Craft knife
◆ Silver sticky tape

Method

1. Select good shaped holly and ivy leaves of a similar size. Trim the stalks and place them face-up on medium weight card, arranging them so they appear to grow from one stem. Hold

TIP:
Many objects can be scanned, so have fun experimenting. Drape a piece of cloth over the top if the lid cannot be closed.

them in place with a small piece of double sided sticky tape. Lay the card face-down on the scanner bed and close the lid gently. Hold the lid down without squashing the leaves.

2. Bring the image on to the computer screen and, if necessary, tidy it up using your painting or image-editing software. Print sheets of multiple images of around 5.5cm (2¼in) each.

3. Cut the card into various sizes and decide on the background papers. Cut or tear them to shape. Make correcting pen dots on the cellophane to represent snowflakes, and cut the holly and ivy images into squares. Put all the background papers face-down into a spray booth and glue. Attach the papers to the cards, then spray glue the holly and ivy shapes and attach them to the cards.

4. The snowflakes are attached on top of the motif and I used silver sticky tape to make borders. One of the cards is made from paper; for added stiffness I used the French fold method (*see* page 12).

DIWALI

The Hindu Festival of Light was the inspiration for these two cards featuring candles. In the first, oil is burned in a clay lamp; the second is a candlestick. Both signify celebration.

You will need

CLAY LAMP

- 29cm x 10cm (11½in x 4in) card with a horizontal fold
- 7 x triangular sequins
- Small piece of rust-coloured paper or card
- Red and yellow felt tip pens

CANDLE

- 21.5cm x 15cm (8½in x 4in) card with a vertical fold
- 4.5cm x 16.5cm (1¾in x 6½in) hologram card
- Round sequins

- Tracing paper
- Rubber-based glue
- Spray glue
- Tweezers
- Magic tape

Method

CLAY LAMP

1.   Trace the flame and clay lamp templates. On the wrong side of the front of the card, draw a light guideline showing the vertical centre. Draw another guideline 4.5cm (1½in) from the base edge of the card. Transfer the flame shape to the wrong side of the front of the card with the base on the guideline.

Using a sharp craft knife, cut out the shape.

2.   Cut a piece of tracing paper to 6cm x 11cm (2¼in x 4¼in), and using the flame shape as a rough guide, colour with felt tip pens. Use red around the outside and fill in with yellow, blending the two so that orange appears. Attach the coloured flame to the wrong side of the front of the card, using dots of glue around the opening.

3.   Transfer the clay pot design to the back of the rust-coloured paper or card and cut out. Glue into place. Using tweezers to hold the sequins, apply glue to the back then attach them to the card to form a line of gold dots at the base of the clay pot.

CANDLE

1.   Draw the smaller flame template on to tracing paper. Colour with felt tip pens as above and cut out. Centre the candle shape on the front of the card and mark with a light pencil guideline. Spray glue the candle and attach it to the card. Add the sequins. Hold the flame in place with a small piece of magic tape cut to fit.

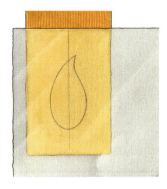

Inside front.

TIP:
Check that the felt tip pens you will be using dry when used on tracing paper. If the ink does not dry, try another brand.

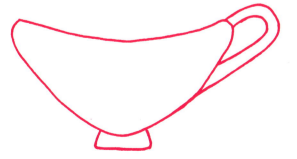

CELEBRATION CRACKER

The tradition of pulling crackers when all the guests are seated around the Christmas dinner table is a great ice-breaker. Hats are donned, the mottoes read and groaned over, and little gifts passed around. This cracker comes in the form of a card, but could also include a motto, gift or crown hat.

You will need

◆ 33cm x 11cm (13in x 4¼in) card
◆ 6.5cm (2½in) square gold paper
◆ 6.5cm x 8cm (2½in x 3in) red mulberry paper
◆ 13cm (5in) long narrow green ribbon
◆ Tracing paper
◆ Sharp pencil
◆ Spray glue
◆ Gold dimensional glitter paint
◆ Craft knife
◆ Steel rule

Method

1.   Score the card 9cm (3½in) from both ends. Trace the template on p. 92 and transfer it to both the mulberry and gold paper. Cut them out. Spray glue all four pieces on the back and attach them to the card, lining up the cracker ends with the scored folds. There will be an overlap where the edges of the card meet. Open the card out flat and trace a zig-zag line on the right-hand edge. Cut out using a sharp craft knife and steel rule.

2.   Close the card with the cut side overlapping and draw the zig-zag shape on to the other edge. Open flat and cut with a craft knife and steel rule.

3.   Add the green ribbon decorations. On the inside of the card, add the glitter spirals.

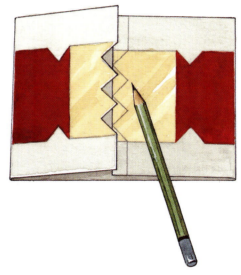

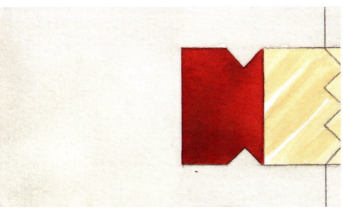

GOLDEN DAYS

A mixture of golden silk and yellow ribbons woven then attached to a backing with beads makes a splendid Golden Wedding card, and can be adapted for a wedding or special occasion by using different colours. The piece can also be made using only ribbons.

You will need

♦ Double fold card with 10cm (4in) aperture
♦ 1.5m of 1cm (1½yds of ⅜in) wide yellow satin ribbon
♦ Strips of co-ordinating silk and lurex
♦ 23 x small beads
♦ 16.5cm (6½in) square of wadding or felt
♦ Masking tape
♦ Double sided sticky tape
♦ Polystyrene tile
♦ Pins
♦ Bodkin
♦ Needle and yellow thread
♦ Scissors

METHOD

1.   Cut ten 14cm (5½in) lengths from the yellow satin ribbon. Cut four 14cm (5½in) lengths of silk and two lengths of lurex, 4cm (1½in) wide. If possible, use pinking shears on the lurex to minimize fraying. Neaten the silk lengths by folding in the cut edges and pressing with a warm iron.

2.   Pin the lengths of narrow ribbon vertically on to the polystyrene tile. Starting with a lurex strip, weave through the vertical ribbons using a bodkin or a plastic tea stirrer. Pin the ends. Add the next strip and continue until the square is complete.

3.   Cut a narrow strip of masking tape and place it on the edges to stop them from shifting. Remove the pins. Place the weaving on top of the wadding and pin each edge. Using yellow thread, sew beads at alternate junctions. Use a tiny stitch to hold the unbeaded junctions in place.

4.   Centre the weaving under the aperture of the card. Lightly mark a register dot in each corner. Neaten the weaving, leaving about 8mm (¼in) outside the register dots. Do not forget to mark the side of the card to be glued down with an 'X'. Attach as shown on page 16.

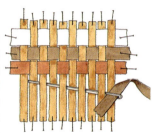

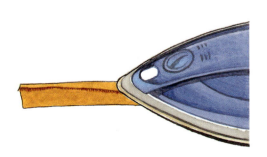

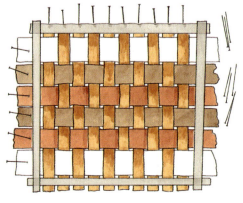

WINTER WREATH

The ivy leaves and winter jasmin flowers in this wreath were collected in my garden on the first day of January. They have not been dried, but pressed on to bonded fabric with a layer of bonded organza on top; miraculously, using this technique, petals and leaves will retain their colour. Machine-embroidery, beads or hand-embroidery can be added to make petal landscapes.

You will need

- 23cm x 18cm (9in x 7in) single fold cards
- 17cm (6½in) square cream backing fabric
- 15cm (6in) square bonding web
- 15cm (6in) square white organza
- 7 x jasmin flowers
- 7 x ivy leaves
- Compass
- Iron
- Pinking shears

Method

1.   Using a compass, draw a light circle guide of 4.5cm (1¾in) radius on to the back of the backing fabric. Protect your ironing board with a piece of sheeting or paper, place the bonding web, sticky side down, over the backing fabric and bond using a warm iron. Leave to cool. Peel off the backing paper.

2.   Arrange the flowers and leaves within the drawn circle. Gently cover with a second piece of bonding web and press the flowers into place with the tip of a warm iron before pressing all over. The flowers might shift slightly, but this does not matter. Peel off the paper when cool.

3.   Place the square of organza over the piece, cover with another piece of used bonding web and press with a warm iron. Leave to cool.

4.   Working from the back, draw another larger circle around the finished piece and cut out with pinking shears

5.   The second motif was made in the same way, using petals from a late-flowering marigold and ivy; however, you can use whatever flowers are available at the time.

STRIPS OF STRIPES

The simple technique of creating stripes and then cutting across them can be used in various ways. Painting straight lines produces a fresh, clean-cut image, while tearing tissue paper and overlapping the edges can be used to evoke landscapes. The strips can be used in small window apertures, as borders, or to decorate envelopes. All of these methods will produce quick results and are suitable for party invitations or Christmas cards.

You will need

◆ Several pieces of cartridge paper
◆ Tissue paper in both light and dark colours, plus silver *or* gouache paints in four or five colours, plus white
◆ 2 x paintbrushes (one thick, one thin) *or* coloured pencils
◆ Cards in a variety of sizes
◆ Silver pen
◆ Adhesive stars
◆ Spray glue
◆ Craft knife
◆ Steel ruler

Method

1.   All paper has a grain so will tear more easily in one direction. Carefully examine (or experiment) to find the best way to tear the tissue paper. Pull off several uneven strips from each colour, varying the widths from about 2.5cm (1in) wide. Overlap the torn edges so that shadows and new colours are created until you are satisfied with the arrangement. Remembering their position, place the strips face-down in the spray booth on a slightly sticky page of the telephone directory. This will stop

them blowing about as you use the spray glue.

2.   Re-arrange the tissue strips on a piece of cartridge paper, cover with a clean sheet of paper and smooth flat. Using a sharp craft knife and steel rule, cut the strips in the opposite direction into various widths and sizes and stick them to the cards.

Below are just some of the ways this versatile technique can be used.

(a)   The triangle card is formed from a diamond shape folded in half.

(b)   1cm (⅜in) strips of the tissue have been used as a border with a detail in the centre.

(c)   The tissue strips have been used vertically on a horizontal fold card.

(d)   A small square aperture with a border worked on the sewing machine (without threading the large size needle), reveals an alternative colour arrangement.

(e)   The painted stripes are cut 1cm (³⁄₈in), 2cm (³⁄₄in) and 4cm (1¹⁄₂in) wide and placed together, but off-set, one in a horizontal arrangement, the other vertical.

(f)   The soft-coloured pencil strip is 4cm (1¹⁄₂in) wide.

TWINKLE, TWINKLE, MANY STARS

This is another versatile technique suitable for Christmas, which can also be adapted using the other templates in the book. Two different coloured cards share a star; the star has been cut from one and attached to the other. Behind the star aperture in the first card, a cellophane square is dotted with white snowflakes and a piece of silver paper pasted to the inside so that it shows through when the card is closed. The cut-out star has fine threads fixed to the reverse and is applied to the second card over a piece of torn tissue paper. The third card is a four-fold card with silver stars on the corners. These are attached separately so that they will tremble and catch the light. I have used the clear plastic top of an old greetings card box, cut into strips, to support the stars.

You will need

- ◆ Several types of card in contrasting colours
- ◆ 5cm (2in) square of cellophane
- ◆ Correcting pen
- ◆ Double sided sticky tape
- ◆ Silver paper or paper sprayed with silver paint
- ◆ Machine-embroidery metallic threads
- ◆ Spray glue
- ◆ Silver paper
- ◆ Cartridge paper
- ◆ Transparent PVC or wire
- ◆ Small piece of card for a template
- ◆ Craft knife
- ◆ Tissue paper

Method

1.   Trace the smaller star template (on page 59) and transfer it to a piece of card. Place the star on the inside left of one of the cards. Draw around the star with a fine pencil. Cut out using a sharp craft knife. Make tiny dots on the cellophane square with a correcting pen and leave to dry. Attach the 'snowflake' square behind the star with a small piece of double sided sticky tape and spray glue the silver paper before putting it on the back right-hand side of the card.

2.   Spray the torn tissue and glue it to the second card. Put a piece of double sided sticky tape on the back of the star. Cut some lengths of thread and lay them over the sticky tape before attaching it to the card.

3.   Cut a piece of card 10cm x 33cm (4in x 13in) and mark with tiny pencil dots at 8.2cm (3¼in) intervals on both sides. Lightly score the centre fold on the reverse and the other two on the right side. The stars need to be double sided, so spray glue silver paper to either side of a piece of cartridge paper. Trace the larger star template, transfer it to the covered cartridge paper then cut out four stars. Cut 5mm (¼in) strips from the PVC or a card box lid and use double sided sticky tape to fix one end of each to a star. Lay the card face-down on an envelope and arrange the stars so that they stand above the top of the card but within the envelope area. Attach the strips to the back of the card.

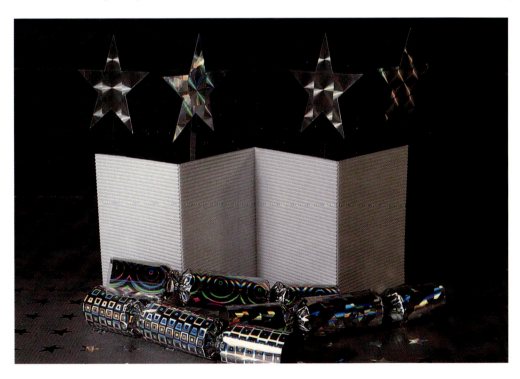

CHRISTMAS TREE

This free-standing Christmas tree can be made from many types of card. The two sides of the tree fold towards the centre forming a stand at the back. Choose from a variety of ways to decorate it.

You will need

- 20cm x 23cm (8in x 9in) bright green card
- Tracing paper
- 20cm x 23cm (8in x 9in) piece of card for template
- Glue
- Adhesive sequins
- Sparkle glue
- Narrow ribbon
- Craft knife
- Adhesive star

Method

1.   Trace out the half-tree template on to the template card, flip it on the centre line and trace the other half. Enlarge it by 110 per cent. Cut it out. Place the cut-out on the back of the green card and draw around the tree branches. Lightly pencil the centre fold line 'A' and turn the card over to mark the two 'B' fold lines on the front. Lightly score the centre line 'A' on the back of the tree with the back of the craft knife. Turn the card over and lightly score the two 'B' fold lines. Erase the pencil lines and concertina the folds.

2.   Working from the right side, spread glue on one side of the centre fold line 'A'. Bring the two 'B' lines together and wait for the glue to dry. When the glue is dry, fold the scored lines so that the tree appears flat with the stand at the back.

3.   Decorate the tree with lines of sparkle glue tinsel, self adhesive sequins, ribbons cut to resemble candles, and so on. The card will fold flat to fit in an envelope, and you could also pop in a self-adhesive star for the recipient to add when the card is standing.

A   B

inside

Fold Line

Templates

Suppliers

UNITED KINGDOM

Art Van Go
16 Hollybush Lane
Datchworth
Knebworth
Herts SG3 6RE
Tel: 01438 814946
Mail order – papers, acrylics and dyes

The Bag 'n' Box Man
Unit 1
West Street
Shutford
Banbury
Oxon OX15 6PH
Tel: 01295 788522
Bags, boxes and packaging materials

Craft Creations Ltd
Ingersoll House
Delamare Road
Cheshunt
Hertfordshire EN8 9ND
Tel: 01992 781900
Paper, cards and envelopes

Creative Grids
PO Box 207
Leicester
Leicestershire LE3 6YP
Tel: 0116 285 7151
Cutting mats

Dylon International Ltd
Worsley Bridge Road
London SE26
Tel: 0208 663 4801
Dyes and sparkle paint

Fred Aldous Ltd
PO Box 135
37 Lever Street
Manchester M1 1LW
Tel: 0161 236 2477
Art and craft materials

Janik Ltd
Brickfield Lane
Denbigh Road
Ruthin
Denbighshire LL15 2TN
Tel: 01824 702096
Craft materials

Maple Textiles
17 Maple Road
Penge SE20 8HT
Tel: 0208 778 8049
Craft materials

Merle's Nimble Fingers
Branscombe
Devon EX12 3AY
Tel: 01297 680322
Découpage papers

Paperchase Products Ltd
213 Tottenham Court Road
London WlP 9AF
Tel: 0207 580 8496
Papers, card and acetate

Tonertex Foils Ltd
PO Box 3746
London N2 9DE
Tel: 0208 444 1992
Pressure-sensitive adhesive and foils

USA

Loose Ends
PO Box 20310
Salem
OR 97307-0310
Tel: 00 1 800 390 9979
Papers and ribbons; Fragment Package containing pieces of papers and ribbons

Sax Arts & Crafts
PO Box 510710
New Berlin
WI 53151
Tel: 00 1 800 558 6696
Paints, papermaking and embossing materials

New York Central Art Supply Co.
62 Third Avenue
New York
New York 10013
Tel: 00 1 800 950 6111
Handmade paper, papyrus and artists, supplies

Decorative Papers
PO Box 749
Easthampton
MA 01027
Tel: 00 1 413 527 6103

SOUTH AFRICA

Art & Graphics Supplies
169 Oxford Road
(Nedbank Centre entrance)
7B Mutual Square
Rosebank
Johannesburg
Tel: 00 27 11 442 9563

X-Press Graph-X
29 Siemert Road
Doornfontein
Tel: 00 27 11 402 4522

Crafty Supplies
32 Main Road
Claremont
Capetown
Tel: 00 27 21 610286

AUSTRALIA

Janet's Art Books Pty Ltd
143 Victoria Avenue
Chatswood
NSW 2067
Tel: 00 61 2 417 8572

Handworks Supplies
121 Commercial Road
South Yarra
VIC 3141
Tel: 00 61 3 820 8399

NEW ZEALAND

Gordon Harris
4 Gillies Avenue
Newmarket
Auckland
Tel: 00 64 9 520 4466

Littlejohns
170 Victoria Street
Wellington
Tel: 00 64 4 385 2099

Index